There Is A Tomorrow

A Collection of Dialogues
In Prose and Poetry
by
John Gilgun
and
Warren Norgaard

For Warren

- John

For John

- Warren

Yes, there is a nirvana; it is in leading your sheep to a
green pasture, and in putting your child to sleep, and in
writing the last line of your poem.

- Kahlil Gibran

All religion, all life, all art, all expression comes down to this: to the
effort of the human soul to break through its barrier of loneliness, of
intolerable loneliness, and make some contacts with another seeking soul, or
with what all souls seek, which is (by any name) God.

- Don Marquis

When you get to the end of all the light you know and it's time to step into
the darkness of the unknown, faith is knowing that one of two things shall
happen: either you will be given something solid to stand on, or you will be
taught how to fly.

- Edward Teller

We have it in our power to begin the world over again.

- Thomas Paine

Introduction

Two years ago, my life seemed ideal. I had a great job with good pay, quality friends, a great apartment in the heart of downtown Phoenix, and a sweet, loving boyfriend – Hugo.

Then, Hugo's mother fell ill. He needed to travel back to Mexico to be with her, while she went through very intense medical treatments. The outcome was unclear, and everyone was worried about her health and future. I wanted to be there for Hugo and his mother; to be at his side, a source of strength and support.

My employer did not approve. Since the Federal Government does not recognize same-sex couples, I couldn't apply for the Family and Medical Leave Act (FMLA). In the end, I chose my relationship over my job. At the time, my heart told me this was really the only choice I had.

A month later, while looking for new employment, I lost my great apartment. In less than two months time, the great job was gone, along with the great apartment. With the apartment, went Hugo. That left only one thing …

… quality friends. Enter John.

John and I have known each other since the early 1990s. The internet introduced us, when we found ourselves members of the same discussion list. As two gay men, the differences in age and geography could not stop our friendship from blossoming.

Over the years, John has encouraged me to create – be it writing, drawing, crafting … or just being. He'd written many poems inspired by various events in my life, and he saw the depression coming over me.

I had moved into my grandmother's then-empty house. Over the years, the condition of this house, in which I still reside, had deteriorated. Holes in the wall, graffiti and shattered windows from area hoodlums, stripped out bathrooms, bad electrical wiring, leaky plumbing – completely overwhelming. It was difficult to come home, day after day, to the living conditions I was enduring. I would think back on my lost apartment, and the depression would set in deeper. I was becoming lethargic, and couldn't find the motivation for daily living.

That's when I got the email from John. His instructions were simple. Collect the poems he had written that related to me, and put them into book format. It would be a part-time project; whenever I got depressed, I could pull out the poems, and get lost in those words.

As usual, it worked. John saved me from my depression. As I put the poems together, I saw one problem. The poems didn't flow, alone. The people who know us and the circumstances surrounding the individual poems, would understand the collection. But to any reader uninitiated to our history and connection, would be lost. The poems needed a point of reference.

It was at this point I went back the beginning. In order for the poems to be cohesive, they needed something more. This prompted me to search through our years of communication, and find the story behind the poems.

The end result is what you find in your hands. Love, compassion, and understanding wrote the words. A creative outlet which saved me from a potentially hazardous depression put them together in a way that makes sense.

What you are about to read chronicles so many things – friendship, love, loss, therapy, writing, and creativity. The text within these covers spans years of dialogue – my trying time attempting to live and love in San Francisco, driving a truckload of slot machines from Phoenix to Northern Minnesota, and moments of love and joy, sorrow and defeat, over many, many years.

In these pages, John and I are stripped naked, for your eyes to view. My hope is that you will walk away seeing the love, compassion, trust, support, and affirmation that exists between two gay men who live thousands of miles away.

I hope you are changed forever, in some positive way, by what you read here. John's job is complete – he has washed away my depression, and left creativity in its place. If you are moved by this book, on any page, or at any moment, then my job is done, as well.

Warren

Orange Cat

Orange Cat slumbers
in the laundry room
gratified by the stench
of unwashed clothing.

This room is secluded
in the corner of the house
only one way in or out.
Here Orange Cat feels safe.

There is a window
overlooking the backyard.
He can perch himself atop the dryer
and survey the outside world
eye the occasional bird
or field mouse
enjoy the thrill of tracking the prey
without the dirty reality of the kill.

Of course, he's only a cat.
He wouldn't consider it
in these terms.

Warren

Of Course He's Only an Orange Cat

Of course he's only an orange cat,
perched on top of the washing machine,
staring out the utility room window at
the flack-flackering birds and the flick-
flickering flies in the oven-deep heat
of the desert garden.

It is a mistake to assume that
he is not aware of that window
or the walls surrounding him, separating him
from his snick-snickering prey--if only
he could get at them, rip them,
shred them, disembowel them with his retractable
claws, his terrifying teeth.

Like the skull under my tensed-up skin,
like the stiffening rope of my backbone,
like the growl from my bottomless gut,
like the 98.9 percent of the genes
I share with the meat hungry chimp --.
He wants -- outside, outside!

John

San Francisco

My Visit with Warren the Wordman in San Francisco

I have a set routine. I take a friend to La Mediterrane, one of my favorite restaurants in San Francisco, and then I show him my favorite places in the Castro/Noe Valley/Mission districts. So I took Warren to dinner at my favorite restaurant and then we walked to a high hill above Mission Park and sat on my favorite stone wall under the pines and amidst the flowers and looked out over what I used to call The City, capitalizing it as a way of saying there is no city on earth superior to it, it is the quintessential city, it is the absolute city, it is--The City!

Well, not quite. Not quite at this point in time. As we sat up there looking down over The Mission, I had to admit that it is now the most expensive city in the world, that no average person can afford to live there, that I've read that something like 400,000 people sleep on the streets there each night, some of them gay kids who fled to the city to escape the oppression in the rest of the country. "What's this city going to be like?" I asked Warren. "I mean, when everyone living here has to be, of necessity, a multi-millionaire, what's going to happen to the shoestring theaters, bookstores, art galleries...? I mean the things that make the place worth visiting?"

Warren said, "There'll be a Recession and the Dot.Commers will go broke and we'll be back to cheap rents again."

But meanwhile, Warren can't wait. In fact, he was leaving the next day, having been unable, like millions of others, to afford to live there, even for a little while.

As we sat there, a young man came up the stone stairs under the pines and crossed over and zeroed in on Warren and started talking. He did not acknowledge my existence. I made the best of it by saying later, "Well, see, this is still a friendly city." But in fact the guy was trying to pick up Warren, I think, because this is not only the most expensive city in the world, it's the loneliest and, well, it's the horniest. Those gay men want intimacy and love--but not quite yet. Or those who really want it can't find it. Or those who find it aren't sure what to do with what they've found it. Or they want a consumer item--buffed, 28 years old, rich, well hung, well connected, nice apartment, nice car, great in the sack, reads GQ, whatever. And if they win this sexual lottery, what then?

Well, the young guy went away. And I walked down with Warren to the park and said goodbye and hugged him. I hugged him and I could feel his ribs through his skin and I thought, "This kid isn't getting enough to eat!"

San Francisco. What a bitch. It'll break your heart. Stay home. At least in Peoria you can get a square meal at Aunt Maud's. At least you won't starve.

John

My Visit with Johnboy in San Fransisco

I always find it interesting to read the other view of a shared experience. I met John at the Inn on Castro, and we walked to La Mediterrane, a wonderful restaurant, and then we walked to the stone wall Johnboy had told me about that overlooks Dolores Park and most of the city as well. It was a wonderful view, but paled greatly to the wonderful conversation Johnboy and I shared there.

I believe the recession will come to San Francisco. I believe the arts will return to San Francisco. I believe it will become, very soon, the place Johnboy remembers it to be.

I find the stranger who approached the most interesting part of Johnboy's story. In total honesty, I found his presence most unwelcome. He was friendly enough, but I felt quite the opposite of Johnboy ... I felt like the invisible one, between the three of us. Most of the conversation took place between Johnboy and the stranger. I was glad to see him take his leave. I felt as if our space had been invaded, in a way ... a deep, personal conversation had to be put on hold for the sake of small talk and pleasantries. So, I was glad to see him take his leave. I was glad to be alone with Johnboy again; for the two of us to share that most personal experience together that is San Francisco.

Warren

My Holy Place

It's above Noe Valley. Turn left on Castro and walk up, up, up. It's a stone wall which looks down into The Mission. Sit on the wall. Open your eyes and look. Close your eyes. Look. This spot is holy to me.

I took Warren Norgaard there. We sat on the wall and talked, surrounded by some of the most expensive real estate on earth. And flowers. And pine trees. We sat there and looked down at the quiet streets of The Mission. A young man appeared in the street under the wall and looked up through the pines and the flowers at Warren and immediately climbed the stairs, went up to Warren and started talking to him.

"You see how friendly people are up here," I said after the young man had left. "He came right up here and talked to you. He was attracted to you."

Warren said, "Yes, but he was annoying. I want to sit up here and talk to you. He got in the way of that."

I sat up here one foggy afternoon in March, 1988. I had met Nikki in Jim Brogan's class in Gay and Lesbian Literature at San Francisco State and I was in love with Nikki. It was more complex than "being in love," however. I had realized early on that as soon as Nikki started to talk about himself, everything he said formed itself into a poem. I was taking a class in Creative Writing with Stan Rice and I told him that my project would be a series of poems about Nikki, who was dying of AIDS. After Jim Brogan's class, I'd sit on the grass outside the Ecumenical House and listen to Nikki talk. We'd drink French Roast coffee, because that got Nikki going. But since he chattered on incessantly anyway, the coffee only opened his floodgates further. Nikki was a Chatty Cathy but everything he said shaped itself into poetry and I'd leave our "French Roast Sessions" and take the Muni back to the Victorian on Capp Street and write another Nikki poem. I had never written poetry before and I was teaching myself to write poetry by turning what Nikki said into free verse poems. Since he was dying, I was also commemorating his life. I thought he'd appreciate this.

He didn't appreciate it. It turned out he hated it and resented me using his life to write poems. He'd phone me and scream at me that I was stealing his life from him. I didn't have his permission to do that. I was a thief. But then the next time we met we'd drink French Roast coffee, have our French Roast time, and the same thing would happen. He'd turn into Chatty Cathy and I'd have another poem. But the phone calls would follow and sometimes they were in the middle of the night and I did, after all, share the place on Capp Street with the volatile and angry man who owned the house and Nikki's crazy calls would wake him up and he'd be furious with me. Nikki also dispatched his boyfriend to San Francisco (they lived in Oakland) to tell me to stop writing poems about Nikki. But I told him I couldn't, which was true. He said I should find someone else to write poems about. I said no one else inspired a poem as soon as he began chattering. There was only one Nikki.

Nikki was not his real name. He told me I could not use his real name in my poems. So I invented the name Nikki. It was a better name anyway. But he still objected. It was close enough to his real name. It was still an act of theft.

Finally I knew I had to break with Nikki. It occurred to me in the middle of one of his tirades over the phone that the virus had attacked his brain and that he was no longer sane. So I walked to the wall above The Mission, my sacred spot, and sat there in silence for an hour, getting over Nikki. There would be no more poems about him. When I realized that I had killed my love for him, I walked down into the Castro, found David Lamble clerking at the Walt Whitman Bookstore on Market and sat with him for the rest of the afternoon, hollowed out emotionally, cold inside, with no other poems to write now, no feelings of love to express, no one's life to commemorate.

I had one more insane phone call from Nikki. I told him, "Don't call any more." He didn't. He died the following December and Jim Brogan took me to his memorial service in Oakland. They passed a teddy bear around the circle and when it came my time to speak, I sat there with the teddy bear in my lap and said, "I loved him. He gave me all those poems. How could I not love him for that?"

John

For Love of San Francisco

I have to say that John is not alone in his love of San Francisco. I fell in love the first night I was there, the first time I stepped out of my vehicle and walked with Israel through Dolores Park, watching the sun set and the fog roll in. There **is** a magic there, just out of reach, even as it affects your every thought, your every move.

In truth, it was my own fault that I did not fare well in San Francisco. For the first time in my life, I turned my power over to someone else. I allowed someone else to be a part in making the decisions that would affect my life. In every relationship prior, I did not permit that release. I did not trust the person enough to allow that to happen. Finally, I had met someone I felt safe with. Someone I believed I could trust. Someone that would let me help them, and at the same time not let anything bad happen to me.

I was wrong. As a result, the city and it's current financial status destroyed me to a point I didn't believe I would ever reach. I didn't tell John at the time, but the meal we shared was my first in almost 2 days. That is why he could feel my ribs when we hugged our goodbyes. I had given up a great deal for Israel. That was a small part of it. For four months, I did not pay credit cards, car payments, loan installments. I bought nothing for myself. I worked two full time jobs, and still couldn't keep up with everything.

After the day with John, I took Israel back to Palm Springs to collect the rest of his belongings. He had taken the money we had saved together to rent an apartment, and given it to someone as a deposit on a room for rent -- for one. I was not welcome. When I brought him back to San Francisco, I had nowhere to go. We had stayed longer than acceptable with my friends there in San Francisco, and I was not welcome where Israel was staying. I spent two nights in my car.

The first night, my car was vandalized while I slept. Someone broke in, and stole from the back area of the car. It is a convertible SUV, so doing so without waking me would not have been difficult.

The second night, I went to a bar. It was the first time I had been to a bar since leaving Phoenix. It was the first time I had consumed alcohol in over 9 months. Now, for those who don't know, gay bars can be dangerous places. A higher-than-usual percentage of bar-related assaults happen in and around gay bars. This has always led me to take certain precautions. The main precaution being that I never, **never**, accept a drink handed to me by anyone other than a bartender. For some reason, on this night, after many, many, many drinks, I broke that rule without even thinking about what I was doing. Less than 20 minutes later, I was getting dizzy, feeling upset to my stomach. I excused myself from the people I had met, and left the bar, to walk down the street the 3 or so blocks back to my car. One of the guys from the bar followed me out, wanting to "walk me home." I told him "Thank you," but informed him that I was involved with someone. He said he understood, and only wanted to see me safely home. I agreed to let him walk me to my car.

At some point before getting to my car, I must have blacked out. I awoke in Dolores Park, having been assaulted, both physically and sexually. Surprisingly, a friend happened to be walking through the park (he is a hustler, so it stood to reason, i suppose), and he took me to a friend's apartment to get cleaned up and to evaluate my condition some.

Now for some of you who have known me for a long period of time, you know this is the second time this has happened to me, although the first time had very different circumstances.

It was many days before I could say in honesty that I was physically "okay." I was hurt, in ways I didn't know I would ever experience. It was then that I realized John's words had more truth than I had realized: "Warren, this city is going to kill you if you don't get out now."

This was when I left San Francisco. I spent one final night in the city, with Israel. His landlord, who I communicate with regularly online now, allowed me to stay, and saw to my condition. I know I will now always be welcome with him, should I ever return to San Francisco.

San Francisco can be an ugly, cruel, and terrifying place. But it can also be magical. I believe, even now, it is magical. At this very moment in time, there are tears streaming down my face as I write this. I am crying for San Francisco. I am crying for Israel. I am crying for the magic. I miss San Francisco. After everything, I miss San Francisco. I yearn every moment to return there. I belong there. In my heart, I can feel that as much as John does. **I belong there.** Not for Israel, or my friends, or any other reason but myself. San Francisco is a part of me, and nothing can change that. I am a part of San Francisco, and nothing can change that, either. With everything that has happened to me, I still see San Francisco as a place of magic, of beauty, of possibility.

I don't know what my future holds, but I know it is held in San Francisco.

Warren

The Boy I Did Not Meet

Because I turned left on 19th and walked up the hill to Eureka,
I did not meet the boy I was destined to meet. His name – Enrico.
I don't know what impulse led me to turn left rather than right,
some nostalgia for the old neighborhood maybe or a sentimental
desire to see Collingwood Park again or some memory of Leonard.

Enrico himself was supposed to meet me on Castro and bump me
in the crowd, his arm against my chest, and in the confusion start
a conversation and we were destined to end up at Starbuck's over
espresso and cookies. That's how the gods had planned it but I
turned left on 19th and walked to Eureka. Leonard lived there once.

Enrico had left his weapon in the glove compartment of the Buick
he had stolen seven hours earlier from the john he spent the night
with over in Marin so I wasn't in any danger of being shot by him.
Not at that exact moment anyway. I was destined to feel sorry for
him as well as loving because I always feel loving. It's my weakness.

I stood by the house where Leonard once lived and stared up at the
kitchen windows, wishing I could turn back time and make it 1980
again and have dinner up there, something with garlic, pasta, chicken.
And Enrico went on into a bar and spent an hour and forty-five minutes
there and left with someone named Cisco and they went to Cisco's place

in the Mission and at this point the gods hit the remote and the screen
goes blank. I should now tell you that I picked up the Chronicle today
and saw Enrico's picture and read about how he'd been convicted of
grand larceny (auto theft) and felt that if I'd met him I'd have liked him.
He was cute in a hip Hispanic way and I'd have enjoyed loving him.

John

Slot Machines: A Journey

On the Road with Warren the Wordman

*I'm leaving this afternoon on a last minute job
driving a truckload of slot machines to Minnesota and...*

It reminds me of Lonely Are the Brave (1962).
Carroll O'Connor in his pre-Archie Bunker days
is driving a rig loaded with toilets through the West
and he runs down the last of the cowboy rebels,
(Kirk Douglas) killing him and his horse.

Someone's waiting in Mankato for those slot machines,
walking over the resilient nap of the red carpet in the casino
in his Tony Lama boots, thinking, "Where's the guy's
supposed to deliver them slots? I need 'em right now."
The first blizzard of the season is chewing up the prairie.

Warren's between Amarillo and Oklahoma City,
off the side of the road near the Cordell/Clinton Interchange.
Stopped to take a piss, which is difficult to do in that wind,
hard even to stand steady, so he's holding onto the fender
with one hand and his Cardinal's baseball cap with the other.
All he's seen for five hours are scattered farms and oil derricks.

And barbed wire fences. Like the one shivering above the ditch,
buffalo grass tossing and twisting in a satanic frenzy.
Then a few yards to the east he sees the coyote hanging
on the wire, someone's shot him and tied him there, or maybe
he ran him down in his truck and then strung him up as a joke.

Jerking back and forth on the wind like that, he looks alive,
as if he were simply caught there on the barbs rather than tied
with baling wire. Warren can see the baling wire twisted around
his throat. He can also see his teeth and his bullet-shaped black
head. Looks like crows have pecked out the eyes. Or maybe the guy

who tied him up there cut them out with a jackknife. Who knows?
Warren zips up and climbs back into the cab. The tape in the tape deck's
playing Ray Charles, A Rainy Night in Georgia. Rainin' all over the world.
But Warren's not alone. Three hours back he picked up a hitchhiker standing
half frozen on an exit ramp, a kid who introduced himself as Sycamore and
fell asleep, his chin on his denim jacket, his knit cap down over his eyes.

He's waking up now though and he says something and Warren says something. And there are a couple of ham sandwiches in a paper bag on the seat and they share that and Warren pops open a beer and they share that and it's not so bad. Life isn't all dead coyotes and blizzards. Handing him the beer

Warren's hand brushes Sycamore's hand and Sycamore stretches his legs, knocking his knee against Warren's thigh. And then he doesn't take it away.

John

Facts about the Truck

It weighs five thousand pounds with its slot machines and in spite of all that weight it rocked back and forth on the blizzard winds in Oklahoma and that made Warren think: oh my.

Slot machines are produced at three factories in Phoenix and the production of the slot machines must be monitored by agents from the gaming commission who live in Phoenix since they need to be near the factories which produce the slot machines. They observe every part of the manufacturing process of the machines in the factory.

Before a truck loaded with slot machines leaves Phoenix it is sealed shut and locked. It can only be unlocked at its destination by someone from the gaming commission, in this case someone who lives up on the Canadian border near a casino on the North Dakota border.

The owners of the factory which produces slot machines pay Warren well and now that he has a steady job he feels he has self worth but regrets the fact that he sometimes has to work fourteen hour days and it leaves no time for creative activity such as writing. Warren meet Al. Al has something to tell you.

Try to imagine a casino in such a remote part of the country. Try to imagine the snow falling for seven months of the year. I once lived in Potsdam, New York, twenty miles north of Tupper Lake, on the Saint Lawrence, where snow started the first week in October was still falling with undiminished intensity in mid- April. Snow by mid-December covered the windows of my bedroom and I lived on the second floor of the house. I did not see clear daylight through those windows for three months. All I saw was banked snow. Try to imagine what it's like in Northern North Dakota.

I assume there are no windows in the casino. You enter the windowless casino out of a snowstorm and park your astrakhan hat, your quilted overcoat, your mittens, your scarf, your overshoes or snow shoes with the young Shoshone woman at the check-in closet. Then you sit down at a slot machine Warren has delivered and put in a fifty cent piece and pull the lever. If the thought crosses your mind, "What does it all mean?" you must repress this thought at once. To attempt to answer the question is to go mad.

More on the truck. Warren must deliver the unloaded truck at a certain place and to a certain person. There's considerable paperwork involved in all this. I don't know if Warren has a security clearance or if he has to be de-briefed but I guess anything is possible. Maybe he has to empty out his pockets to prove he hasn't stolen a slot machine. Once he gets through this process, he intends to rent a pickup truck and drive back to Phoenix. Warren has never been east of El Paso so this is the first time he's seen Amerika. It is extraordinarily flat and empty and the wind--well, the wind blows and blows.

There are people in Amerika and they gather at places called Ma's Pies and drink coffee and bullshit together and they all have large dogs and ham-sized butts which fit with an oomph and a grumph on the stools at the counter and when Warren walks in out of the snow seeking shelter they give him only one quick glance and then go back to the conversation they were having about how hard it is to understand women and how you can't live with 'em or without 'em and haw!

John

Small White Wolf

Somewhere in western Minnesota I saw a small white wolf
by the side of the road, standing over a dead doe,
and my impulse was to stop the truck, get out,
and shout at him, "Get away! Leave her alone."
I was already a day late with my delivery
and it would have been ridiculous to stop
to disturb what was, after all, only nature.
We all have to eat, after all. Get real.
But then I found myself pulling off the road,
getting out and going back, though it was
fifteen below zero, five in the morning.
blowing snow, frostbite country.

The moon was in its final quarter,
the lower part lit, the upper part
blue-black, setting on the horizon
of the prairie I'd been staring at
through the windshield for hours--
no trees, just a sea of grass.
Not a moon to give much light,
yet as I approached the wolf
I could see that its body
was radiant with moonlight
and I remember thinking,
"The wolf is not white at all.
It's the moonlight on its fur."

Nor was it a wolf.
Or rather, it was a wolf for a second,
but then it transformed itself into a man.
And the doe was not a doe
but an old woman crouching in the grass.
Each watched me warily. Neither spoke.
Then I felt myself being transformed as well--
my soft radiant skin, my mirroring bones, my teeth.
"This is sexual," I thought.
And the woman, who could read my thoughts, said, "Yes, it is."

John

God is a Black Bean

Warren the Word Man called yesterday from Kansas City where he spent Monday night. He is on an epic American journey, transporting a truck filled with slot machines from Phoenix to Minnesota. I had assumed he was going to Albert Lea or Mankato or Minneapolis, which would mean a straight shot up I-35 from Kansas City to Des Moines to Minneapolis. To get to Joetown he would have to go thirty-eight miles out of his way. I suggested that he stop in Gallatin to see Ed and Jesse, since Gallatin is right off I-35, and skip his visit to me, given the weather and the fact that he is already a day behind in delivering the slot machines. He told me he was going to far western Minnesota on the South Dakota border, not to Minneapolis, and that he would travel on I-29, there being no other way to get to that part of the country, and I-29 brings him directly to Joetown. Years ago Palmer Hall visited me here on his trip to Fargo, North Dakota. And W. Scott Olsen, who lives up there, also stopped to see me once, on his way home from a conference.

So I gave him directions to my house from Exit 50 on I-29 and waited for him. An hour later he phoned and told me he'd found my street, Rock Springs Road, but the truck was so large it wouldn't fit on that street and he'd driven back to the Belt. I think he was phoning from Rinky Dink Gas and Convenience on the corner of the Belt and Blackwell. So I told him to park the truck in the Wal-Mart parking lot near the mailbox and I'd be up there in a few minutes to pick him up in my car and bring him to my house.

Which I did.

I'd prepared lunch and after a tour of the house--this house which is a living history museum of my life, filled with art, books, and everything I put into my poems each morning (the sliding glass door, the deck, the spruce tree, the redbuds, the sweetgum, etc.) --we ate. While he was eating he told me he'd given my poem about God--"God is a black bean"--to a Christian Fundamentalist friend (I think he also said this friend was a gay boy) "as a way of helping him." And I said, "Well, you can tell him that you ate God while you were here because those Progresso Black Beans are what you are eating now." Ha.

It's true. Come to Joetown and eat God--in a black bean.

This was our second face-to-face (Warren and myself, not myself and God) and the other one was in San Francisco last summer. Last summer he was hungry and desperate and on his way out of The City because, like millions of others, he could not afford it--financially, emotionally, existentially, and romantically. This time though Warren was centered, whole, and confident, on top of things. I said, "You've grown up." I was impressed this time by his intelligence. I thought that this intelligence came across as bright, sharp and clear--like stainless steel. But now I think it also came across like something sharp and clear out of the brass section of an orchestra. It was wonderful to experience that. And, also, there were things I could relate to as a gay man because I was 28 once myself and I too reached a point at that age where I began to understand relationships and power issues and control problems and what love may really mean. (It's not an MGM musical from the 1940's. Surprise!)

We also talked about the importance of creativity and I told him he had this epic journey to write about and that should give him material to write about for the next six months. "Post what you write to the Lists."

I am committed to helping gay men. This is one of the things Gay Liberation is all about. But Warren has figured out things for himself and doesn't need help. Still, I showed I was here if he needed support. I related to him as an older brother. We have things in common, family issues. The connections between us are powerful.

After he had eaten I gave him his poem, the one written for him, "On the Road with Warren the Word Man," which was also an act of support and love, and drove him to the Wal-Mart parking lot and he took off in his truck. Before he got out of my car I hugged him and said, "I'm glad you're doing well. It means a lot to me that you're doing so well." Look, this is what you do as a gay man. This is how you act. Deliberate acts of kindness. Being fair, being decent. Actions have consequences: act out of friendship and love. Have the courage to actually care. It's scary, I know. But — care! Bitchiness is out. Caring is in.

Sometime in the evening I surfed the television and here was Dan Rather and it was a Special Report on what the three stooges on the Supreme Court had handed down to us--Larry Thomas, Moe Rehnquist and Curly Scalia-- and there was now not a single branch of our government which had not disgraced itself and which could be treated with respect. This on top of the fact that the fundamental act at the center of the republic had been discredited--I mean, the very act of voting. Awesome! For weeks friends have been telling me that I'm over-reacting. "We are not in a crisis situation, etc." Listen. We are in a crisis situation and its the most dangerous situation a democracy can be in--a crisis of belief. I'm not Cassandra telling you something you don't need to believe from the walls of Troy. But what I thought was, "Americans are a people who are fundamentally decent and deserve better than this." I thought of Warren but then I also thought of Ed and Jesse and others. There is a fundamental "rightness" in the center of my people and they deserve better. I thought, "Well, if every institution on the federal level has been discredited, we have the state governments, so we can fall back on that." But then I thought, "No, forget that. We have each other. We have each other and we can treat each other with respect and deliberate acts of kindness and support and love. Yes." And I did that and it was a good day and I fell asleep at eleven o'clock feeling good about myself and about my people.

Reach out to someone today and indicate to them that you care about them. Do it.

I care about Warren.

End of report.

John

The Life of the Mind

"The life of the mind is enough." Well, there's also the life of the heart and I talked about this with Warren the Wordman during his visit, also. I said to him, "You can't have sex with all the people you love. You have to find other ways to love them. You teach them if you're a teacher. You do art with them if you're an artist. You write books with them and sculpt with them and do poems with them. You create a body of creative work using any media available to you, including the internet, and you celebrate the lives of the people you love and that's your legacy and what more do you need?"

I also told him something that he could see all around him in this house, that is that this house is a celebration of the people I have loved here. It is a memorial to life and loving moments and communion and fellowship and community. Jeff, you painted this house, you put the roof on, you and Roger did the deck. I live in the center of these continual acts of kindness and human decency. The warmth that allowed us to sit in this house was coming up through the furnace because you told me to call Webb the Furnace Man!

"It begins with Larry Williams in 1973 and here are his drawings on the wall. And it goes on. And there's a story attached to each picture, to each pot, to each piece of furniture, to each bowl. Everything has a history here in this house. And it is a history of love. It is a history of friendship and support and comradeship. It is a history of defying all the odds and winning."

Warren said, "We don't have this in Phoenix. We don't have this community. We don't have this sense of connection. You have it here. We don't have Ed and Jesse. We don't have a community like Gallatin."

I said, "You come back in the spring. I want to introduce you to Dooley and to Hans and to Roger and to Jeff. I want you to be part of this community. You are part of it. You are in the center of it now. You will always be part of it. Come back and see the flower gardens and Dooley's kiln and the farmhouse where Hans lives and see the way our art, our poetry is all over this place. Come on a first Friday and get up and read your poems. Feel that sense of incredible connectedness. That's life. And it's all built on friendship and love. And it is life-lasting. And we have it here. And it's not in Tucson where people just pass through. And it's not in Phoenix where people don't know their neighbors and walk around lost and lonely and afraid. It's here. Hey, Warren! I'll pick you up at KCI!"

When the life of the mind is also the life of the heart, what more do you need?

John

Defining Your Home

I've read the attached post from John probably 20 times since I returned from my trek across the states. I have to agree, teary-eyed, with every word. I create with, for, and because of the people I love. At times, I create in spite of them, too. I am overcome with a desire to create. For Christmas, I got the stained-glass crafting tools I need to start doing more stained-glass work. I started that before I went to SAN FRANCISCO, and I loved it. I loved the way it felt to create some*thing* ... something I could hold in my hands that was more than a piece of paper. Perhaps, when I have a book of writings together, I will feel that way about my poetry, as well.

I think about the idea of John's home ... and the creations which envelop him on a daily basis. Much of what I have on my walls was bought. Two Mapplethorpe prints, a few inspirational pieces, a Salvador Dali print. And two masks, made by John. I have one of John's poems on my wall, now, as well, next to one of the masks, the first mask he gave to me, which hangs just to the right of my computer, watching me as I type. It inspires me. It is not a full house, but it is a beginning of one.

I also think about the lack of creative community here in Phoenix, and I know that I am wrong. It does exist here, but in a different way. I was a part of it, once upon a time. Back when I was doing poetry readings, participating in Poetry Slams, spending time at the coffeehouses. We would meet in basements in downtown Phoenix at 10 and 11 pm and do poetry slams. They were as underground as illegal parties used to be. It was as if we were on the lam, hiding out from the conformity police, and it was grand. It is still there, I know. I get tidbits of info through the grapevine. But I stop myself from going. I don't know why. Perhaps I will, again, very soon.

Returning to Missouri again in the early spring sounds wonderful, and it is something I am looking forward to greatly. I am getting a group of friends together for mid-March, when we are going to jump from a perfectly good airplane, and pay for the privilege. It was one of my resolutions this year: to do one thing which terrifies me. I am doing two. I am also spending this year alone. By alone, I mean without romantic tangles, so that I may find my focus, find my chi again, and create. It is in there, I just need the focus back to tap into it, and bring it out again.

Warren

Something's Happening

"Even when nothing's happening, something's happening."
--A Joetown koan.

Not too much is happening and not too little is happening. It is not too hot and it is not too cold. It is not too soft and it is not too hard. It is just right. I have lived here for 28 years and I have said too often, "Nothing ever happens here!" Just yesterday the thought crossed my mind that it is a shame that I have never been able to afford to live in a major American city for any appreciable length of time. Even when I had the money to do it, as I did after 1987, I didn't have the money to do it. For decades I have put myself to sleep with the fantasy that some billionaire has willed me a house on Steiner Street in San Francisco and the million dollars a year which would allow me to live in it comfortably. I tell myself, "You want to be a writer who has an effect on American culture and you have never been rich enough to live in a major American city." I look at the cultural sections of the three gay papers I receive each week and say, "Here are a hundred movies and plays I will never see. Here are a dozen concerts I will never attend. Here are art exhibits I'll never go to and cheese I'll never nibble and wine I'll never drink and crackers I'll never crunch and conversations I'll never have with artists and gallery owners."

Now I am sixty-five years old and the answer comes to me. This is the perfect place to be. Why? Because so little happens here that everything happens here. To be specific, one visitor arrives once every six months and sits on the couch in the living room and talks to me and then leaves. I wake the next morning and write a poem about the visit. Warren the Word Man arrives and talks and departs and a series of poems are produced about that. Mike Swope arrives and talks for an hour and a half and a poem comes out of that. I get invited out once a year (to Jeff's mother's house on Christmas Eve) and "Opening the Magic Set on Christmas Eve" comes out of that and it takes only twelve minutes to write. One breakfast with Ed and Jesse at Perkin's leads to several poems. Greg Louganis comes to give a talk and I go to the Missouri Theater for the first time in fifteen years and three poems come out of that. I see Dooley once a month and a poem comes out of that--always, invariably. I can count on it.

Absolutely!

I don't rush from experience to experience. There aren't that many experiences. I have an experience on Tuesday and write about it on Wednesday, Thursday and Friday. When I have contemplated each aspect of this experience, I feel I have lived it. Plus there it is--in the language of the poem. It's there forever, like a fly trapped in amber.

I then get the poems to the people who contributed to the experience and their lives are enhanced. I have established "community" and I have strengthened it. "Here is a poem about our experience together." This action dispels any loneliness I might feel, though, in fact, I either never experience loneliness, though I am alone 90 percent of the time, or if I do experience it I don't recognize it as loneliness. At the moment of writing the poem I am with all the people I love. At the moment of e-mailing them the poem I am with them. At the moment of reading the reply, I am with them. I am with them in my mind. I am truly with them. This "with" doesn't roll off me like water. This "with" is fixed there forever. It is in the poem.

I have transformed our experience through my art and created with my friends a community (Buddhists call this a "sangha," a community) and I feel fully alive in mind, spirit and body. I feel totally in touch with things. I am not alienated from experience. I have made the experience our own special experience through my art. I have as much time as I want for contemplation. I have silence. If a poem arrives at one in the morning, I can get up and write it. I can't disturb anyone. There's no one here to disturb. If I have to sit here all night until I get the poem right, I can sit here all night until I get the poem right. No one wakes and looks at the other pillow and asks, "Where's John?"

This contemplative time has a name. Mayo Denis Lacey calls it "turning the light around." A person "turns the light around" when he dispels the distractions of life and "gets to the heart of things." It's Buddhist meditation but it's not sitting on a pillow humming to myself. It's taking the experiences of my life and, in isolation and in silence, transmuting that experience into a poem. I can't imagine doing this in New York City, for instance, where the person who lives upstairs is almost ready to drop his other shoe onto the floor at four a.m. but doesn't do it and someone screams in the street and a plane takes off from JFK and the sonic boom shakes the lamp on the bedside table. If I lived in such a place I might long for Joetown where, because nothing ever happens, everything takes on meaning--the feeling of the cord on my fingers as I open a drape in the living room at seven o'clock to let the light in or the sound of a single snowflake falling on a dry brown leaf of the pin oak in the front yard at eight. These things echo in eternity. Well, not always. But sometimes. Often enough to make it worthwhile. Often enough to make them worth writing about.

It is difficult to write this and not make it sound as if I'm merely compensating for an empty life. But it's not compensating. And it's the opposite of an empty life.

John

Snowed In

I woke at 4:30. For the first time in many months, it proved impossible to write a Daily Poem. After an hour and half of trying to do it and failing, I went back to bed and slept for another two hours. It is now eight in the morning CST, Saturday.

Warren the Wordman phoned about seven last night and said he was giving up and checking into a motel in Des Moines. The roads are already ice-slicked in Iowa and the window of his rented car continually fogs up so that he can't see out. He dropped off the slot machines in North Dakota, rented a car and drove to Minneapolis, where he stayed with a relative. He intends to come here to Joetown, meet up with Ed and Jesse and drive later to Kansas City International to catch a flight to Phoenix. I begged him to stay in Des Moines until the blizzard passes. Weather Channel says this is a major killer storm. Yet I woke a few minutes ago to find that the snow has apparently melted off my street, which was snow-packed yesterday, and except for the fact that the strong winds are moving the bare limbs of the redbud trees, there is no evidence at all of a storm here in Joetown. I asked Warren to phone Larry in Des Moines and gave him the phone number. Then I phoned Larry who told me that because of serious problems at his house involving his housemate Edful and because of his own health problems he can't invite Warren over. I told him to talk to him over the phone if he called. If the blizzard is as bad as the Weather Channel tells me, Warren won't be able to get over there from the motel anyway. And yet the Weather Channel can make a simple winter storm seem like the end of the world sometimes so who can tell? There is an advisory down here. People are being asked to stay off the roads. Kansas City is experiencing problems with car wrecks on ice-covered roads. I haven't been able to get to the post office or the cafeteria for five days. I tried yesterday but freezing fog and rain coated the windshield before I got to the bottom of my street so I turned around and drove right back home and put the car in the garage. I have enough food to last me in here and the mail can wait. Dooley phoned last night to ask me if I had heat or needed anything and I have both heat and food. I thought it was nice that he phoned. I have not even experienced cabin fever yet. I'm OK.

John

Frozen

Frozen street at frozen sunrise through a frozen window:
a piano keyboard with white keys only, no black keys,
frozen notes, frozen jazz, cream white frozen fingers sus-
pended in frozen air like frozen clouds over frozen Kansas.

I walk from room to room, Omar Sharif in Doctor Zhivago,
and with a single finger I trace a circle on a window so cold
the hairs on the back of my hand spring to attention like
uniformed sentinels guarding the entrance to Prague Palace.

They say this is the blizzard of the century but only forty
flakes of snow fell yesterday on the deck, I counted them,
standing at the sliding glass door, staring out at the red cedar
tossing in the wind. Is this the fifth, sixth or seventh day of this?

Warren the Wordman is trapped in a motel in immobile Des Moines,
a placid, quintessentially American city where every road ends
in a shopping mall and every restaurant begins with a salad bar,
seven kinds of Jell-O, nine varieties of pasta and ranch dressing.

My hope is that he has found a boyfriend there and that they are in bed
under the peppermint comforter beneath the picture of a deer drinking
from a stream under a willow--though finding a boyfriend in at motel
in Des Moines... But anything is possible when you're 28 and cute.

What happened to the greenhouse effect? Is the Royal Penguin
on Macquarie Island no longer endangered? Have the Discovery
people gathered in Vienna to shred their scripts? Is Vatnajokull
still Europe's largest ice sheet? Perhaps it's even expanding,

swallowing up ski lodges, Volkswagens, knit caps, Visa cards?
Meanwhile in the austere, severe sky off the coast of southern Chile
a Pink-footed Shearwater circles on slow wing beats, dreaming
of fish and the Southern Hemisphere and he couldn't care less.

                                                                John

Arrival

Warren the Wordman did finally arrive here at my house from Gallatin (where he was at Ed and Jesse's house). He didn't arrive when I thought he would arrive and I was worried and phoned Ed about it. I worried because he could have lost his way, though this seemed impossible given the fact that Warren has been here once before and the fifty miles from Ed's house to mine is so simple, you only have to make about three turns! It's more or less a straight shot from there to here. But finally he did show up. He had stopped to get something to eat.

We sat up till about eleven talking in the living room. There are things about him which remind me of myself when I was 28. So I can relate. About quarter till eleven he had begun to yawn so I suggested he pack it in. He's in the guest room now sleeping. It's 7:50.

I'm pretty good at description but I don't think I want to describe how bad things are here in terms of weather conditions. I haven't been outside in almost a week. I just looked out and down into the driveway and Warren's rented car is covered with the snow that fell last night. If we can do it, I will take him to Jerre-Anne's World Famous Cafeteria today. I don't know but the weather is getting to me. I woke about three and the house was cold and I imagined a pipe had broken in the intense cold (hardly possible since the house is built so that all the pipes are in the central core of the house, protected from cold) but I was so anxious and tense that I walked through the house trying to reassure myself that everything was all right in here. If the furnace breaks down, we are in very big trouble. But it's basically a brand new furnace since I had to have a new motor put in a few months ago and it is functioning valiantly. But, my God, I have never experienced such cold in Missouri! I want to take this opportunity to thank Jeff who got me a furnace man last October, a man named Webb who put the new motor in. This weather is more like Fargo than Joetown.

It is good to have a guest under these circumstances. Warren leaves at two this afternoon from Kansas City International Airport, if planes are taking off there. Where is Global Warming now that I need it? What happened to Al Gore's "Global Warming is real!" One should never make such an assertive statement particularly when it concerns weather. Watch y' mouth nex' time, Al Gore.

John

These Things Are To Be Praised

The way the blizzard wind
smoothes the footprints in yesterday's snow,
but doesn't erase them, not quite, no,
and I think, "That's a metaphor
for memory and for death, because we
never quite forget and we never quite die,
because our friends remember us and mourn us
and celebrate our lives by putting us in their poems."

The way Jesse went to the microphone
in the Missouri theater and asked Greg Louganis,
"How can I come out to my parents?"
And it was like strong music, like Shostakovich.
And how Louganis said, "My god is a loving god."
And how the wind tries to erase
the crusted ridges in last week's snow
and how it fails at that and how I go on remembering.

The way Warren, who'd been sitting up real straight
and very much the mature adult, talking about how
he had a job now, was paying his bills, was
oh so responsible, had a backbone you couldn't
put your hand through, as Thoreau might say,
suddenly leaned sideways and was transformed
into a laughing boy alive with a childlike delight,
and I said, in celebration, "That is so beautiful!"

And the way Mike said, speaking out of an inner rage,
"I will have passion in my life, I will have a creative life."
And how nothing can ever erase the will to live.
And how that will is like a mirror illuminated from within.
And how we step inside and there's a fierce spirit there.
And how this spirit holds out its hands to us,
the way our fathers did when we were learning to walk,
and says, "That's right. Come to me. I'm here."

John

The Essential Boy Shines Through

When Warren Norgaard visited me on his trip to Minnesota in midwinter to deliver slot machines to an Indian reservation, he was sitting on my sofa talking to me, all grown up and formal and adult. Then suddenly, apparently without thinking about it, he picked up a pillow and hugged it to his chest. I said, "I hug pillows that way, too." Suddenly the adult Warren vanished from his face and "the essential boy" shone through. It was as if a mask had dissolved and the face of the original boy was there, in the smile, in the eyes, in the entire face.

At the Belvedere, that great rambling queer construction on the shore of Fire Island with its towers and minarets and campy statues in courtyards, Jerry was sitting on the floor of my room by a chest of drawers. I forget what he was saying and I forget what I was saying. It wasn't something as visual and memorable as Warren hugging a pillow to his chest. But suddenly the adult Jerry vanished from his face and "the essential boy" shone through. When it happens it always amazes me. I know it when I see it. It's a surprise and it's a great joy. It is a revelation. I've seen the essence of the man and he's still a boy inside. "A thing of beauty, and a boy forever." It's Platonic.

Mark Doty brought his 17 year old dog to his reading because the dog at such an advanced age can't be left behind when Mark goes somewhere. So the dog was there in the Wesleyan Music Hall as Mark stood at the podium and read his poems. The dog took over the whole reading because no one could pay attention to Mark as this dog wandered around and barked (always at the climax of each of the poems Mark was reading) and lapped Mark's hand and made friends with a poodle some woman brought in on a leash. In spite of this Mark remained a professional adult poet reading his poems and ignoring his dog. Finally he said, "I guess I'd better read a poem about my dog." The poem was about the death of this dog which will happen soon since the dog is so old and at one point in the poem Mark almost broke down and cried. At that moment the professional adult poet vanished and the eternal boy shone through. It was so absolutely real and so moving that when he finished his reading I went up and introduced myself and shook his hand. I wouldn't have done this otherwise. Why shake hands with a professional adult robot poet doing his scheduled thing for pay, a thing he has done hundreds of times before? But how can you not shake the hand of a man who has revealed himself as the eternal child he is inside?

When the real boy shines through it is--oh so totally Zen!

While I was in Middletown I purchased Letters to J.D. Salinger edited by Chris Kubicka and my friend Will Hochman (University of Wisconsin Press) and I also purchased a book by Salinger's daughter, a memoir of her life with Salinger. Because of this, it flashed on me that this "shining through of the essential child" is pure Holden Caulfield. This is Phoebe on the carousel in Central Park, this is the nuns with their woven baskets in Grand Central collecting coins, this is that girl who keeps her checkers in the back row, this is "Where do the ducks go in the winter when the pond in Central Park freezes over?" I realized that though I read The Catcher in the Rye at sixteen when it first came out, I am still Holden inside at sixty-six, fifty years later. I am still waiting for Phoebe to raise her fingers at that Hitchcock film The 39 Steps (?) just at the moment the villain raises his and in the same way. (He has lost his middle fingers so Phoebe keeps her middle fingers pressed against her palm.) This shining through of the essential child is what Holden is losing at his age and this is what made that novel so meaningful to me at sixteen because I was losing it, too. I too was evolving into an adult phony. But in fact I realize now at 66 that I didn't lose it. I fought every day of my life to retain it. They don't call me "Johnboy" for nothin'! Whee! "I don't want to grow up!" "Peter Pan on the Island of Lost Boys forever!"

Since Warren, Jerry, Mark Doty and myself are gay men, I asked Robin is she ever sees this shining forth of "the essential boy" in straight men. She said she does but less often than in gay men. She said that her Japanese husband has this essential boy right there at all times and it is always coming through (even though the Japanese are so reserved--at least officially) and that this ability to laugh and be a boy is one of the reasons she loves him. She showed me a photo of him holding up a sushi and laughing and said, "This is it." Beside him his son who was about five at the time is laughing uncontrollably at his father holding up a sushi that way and I said, pointing to the son, "That's the look!" Robin's husband is an artist, a printmaker. Of course. How can you be an artist without having that "essential child" right there and at the ready at all times? That's where your creative energy is invested--in that essential child.

I also asked Robin if she ever saw this "look" in women and she said, "Yes, when girlfriends laugh or giggle together. It comes through then."

I also asked a man at the conference about all this and he said immediately, spontaneously, "I teach kindergarten kids and there are some that either never had that innocence or have lost at by the age of five." And I asked myself, "Are there infants born without it?" You tell me.

John

Winter

A Visit To Joetown

It was a short journey,
looking back,
almost as though from bedroom
to balcony,
before I saw the sign
pointing me toward Joetown --
St Joseph, straight down,
Rest of the world, keep on driving.

It was there I found
Johnboy
LeDeck
MoWo
Eddie
and the
Edge City Poets.

It was not as I expected,
with its radio waves spewing
Poet Laureate after Poet Laureate,
its street sides littered with
the most astonishing masks
full of emotion, and stories
most didn't stop to hear.

The words of Johnboy's
retirement speech
still linger in the air
here, in **this** place.

The waters are thick
with the motivation and
compassion of the multitudes
of Joetown educators
which has somehow drained
from years of suspect neglect
and gradually slipped away
as they showered each morning
while the sun rises.

Warren

Make It Hot

It is 10, 20, perhaps 30 below zero here at four a.m. Do me a favor and write a poem about "hot"--chili peppers, a beach in Jamaica in July, hot springs in Yellowstone, anything! As long as it's hot!

John

December in Phoenix

Right now,
in St Joseph, Missouri,
it is twelve degrees
below zero.

Meanwhile,
one thousand
two hundred
and eighty six miles away
in Phoenix, Arizona,
it will reach
seventy two degrees
by mid-day.

Today,
in St Joseph, Missouri,
John will write a poem
drink some coffee
and freeze his proverbial balls
while stepping out onto
Le Deck
to count snowflakes
that won't fall,
he will rediscover a book
on a shelf in his living room,
and he will inspire us
to greatness.

Meanwhile,
one thousand
two hundred
and eighty six miles away
in Phoenix, Arizona,
I will slide into a pair of walking shorts
a *someone-look-at-me* t-shirt,
a pair of drugstore flip-flops,
and my trademark navy blue ball cap.
I will drive to nameless
shopping mall number eighty four
with the windows rolled down
warm air engulfing me,
rushing up my shorts making my balls sweat.

_____

I will pass through an Arizona Christmas
with Saguaro Cacti drowning in blinking lights,
Southwestern Nativity Scenes
complete with blinking chili pepper festivities,
and on one local roof I will spy
– and be revolted by –
the jolly image of St Nick
complete with cowboy hat.
I will come home exhausted from a day of
cold consumerism,
sit at my computer,
and read an email John will send me.
And I will be inspired.

Warren

The First Three Minutes of My Day

I put on a sleep mask and walk through my house.
I want to experience my home through my fingertips.
I touch the wallpaper which is made up of millions
of threads of bamboo, raised highways radiating out
through the central nervous system of this house,
horizon lines extending into infinity, never meeting.

My fingertips encounter the glass of a picture, smooth,
cool, like the back of a bather emerging from the waves
on an Atlantic beach, Revere or Lynn or Marblehead.
Warren the Wordman said this is the house of an artist
and my fingers have come in contact with a framed poster
given to me by a clerk at Blackwell's Books in Oxford.

I know the poster reads Pride 98 and was used to promote
Gay Pride Week and when the week was over no one
had a use for it and I asked for it and it was given to me,
the way the British will give you things if you ask, why not?
So take it, luv, and give it a good home with our blessing.
And now my fingers take in an entire wall of art work

and I'm on the stairs, my toes experiencing the wool carpet,
and the fingers of my left hand touching the railing, which
is like a slide at an amusement park, all down down down,
and swift as ice to a hockey puck or red runners to a sled.
And now I'm in the living room and it's colder down here,
heat rises, my fingers on the nubbly cord that opens the drapes

and this is one of the joyous moments of the morning, because,
though I cannot see it, light floods through the room, light from
the wintery sun, touching Dooley's oil painting over the fireplace,
and his pots and Larry's flower arrangement and the couch
and the coffee table with letterpress books by Gerald and Robin.
New millennium, new century, new year, new day. And I'm still here.

                                                                    John

A New Beginning

I awoke to a new day. A new year. A new decade. A new century. A new millennium. A new beginning.

I did not stay up for the festivities, for the countdown. I did not sit in front of my television and watch Dick Clark refuse to retire. I did not get drunk, did not kiss anyone at the stroke of midnight, did not celebrate. I have an entire year to celebrate. A decade, a century, a millennium, a *lifetime* of celebration ahead. So why sacrifice sleep?

So at midnight, I was asleep, restful, peaceful. This is a good way to start this new journey -- well rested, invigorated, prepared.

At 7am this morning, I awoke from a dream of the beach. Specifically, a dream I have experienced in regular intervals, across many years. I am standing on a rock formation just off the coastline south of the Ocean Beach Fishing Pier, in San Diego, California. I am standing on this rock which appears to have rising from the very ocean, just barely peaking out over the ebb and flow of the tide, and I am looking out at the ocean, surrounded by water, my arms outstretching in each direction to my left and right, Christ-like. I am being cleansed.

I have this dream whenever it is time for me to cleanse myself, spiritually, emotionally, mentally. When things are too cluttered, or need to be put behind me, this is my journey. I will get up and I will go to San Diego, and I will stand on the rock, and I will feel the tide pull away the negatives and reinforce me with an overwhelming feeling of new life coming over me, filling me. It is symbolic, of course, but beautiful and necessary, nonetheless.

When I woke from this dream, I wish I could say that my first thought of this new era was, "This is my new beginning." It was not. My first thought was that Jesse has never seen the ocean. My second thought was that I want to show Jesse the ocean. I want Jesse to stand on that rock, and experience for himself what he would probably describe as my God-experience. My third thought was, "This is my new beginning."

Why did I think of Jesse? I don't know. Will I ever get the opportunity to show him that spot, to show him the Pacific Ocean? Probably not. But there it is. There is so much that Jesse has not seen. There is so much that I have not seen. There is so much that many of us have not seen, may never see. I want to see it all. I want to experience it all. I want to learn it all. I want to *love* it all.

But reality tells me this may not happen. I will not dwell on that. I will dwell on what can happen. This coming weekend, I will drive to San Diego, and I will stand on that rock, in the cold, and I will feel cleansed. I will feel peace. I will feel calm. I will feel renewed. To some, I will feel God.

Warren

Love

Perhaps You Didn't Notice ...

> "If you ever came on to me I'd probably
> melt like an ice cube." - *John Gilgun*

It's been ten years now.
From 1390 miles away,
We made love. But,
Perhaps you didn't notice.

It was discreet, I'll admit.
Intercourse, through email,
Penetration via modem.

I stripped you naked,
One word at a time,
Slowly, sensually,
Kissing your skin
With every keystroke.

We've been going at it
For ten years now,
As hot and heavy
As that very first time. But,
Perhaps you didn't notice.

Once, I sat across from you
In your living room,
On your couch,
Hugging your pillow
To my body
As we conversed
So passionately.

For a moment that night,
When your eyes sparkled,
Vibrant and excited,
And your smile widened
Encompassing the room,
You were twenty again.
We made love in that moment
And it lasted for days. But,
Perhaps you didn't notice.

Warren

_____

I Wake

I wake at four in the morning to Warren's poem. What can I do, waking to a poem as good as this poem, except write my own poem in reply to it? Has anyone else ever been roused into waking consciousness by a poem sent via e-mail like this? Ah, brave new world, to have such technology in it! A love poem via e-mail at four a.m. demands a love poem in return.

John

Backstory

Perhaps you don't remember.
It's been 1,390 years now.
Yes, it happened in a previous incarnation,
in the port city of Valletta on the island of Malta.
Your name was Glicine, which you pronounced "gleecheenay,"
and which means, in Italian, wisteria,
the vine, the purple flower, like your cock unfolding
in the morning light, light which spread across the narrow bed,
across the blanket embroidered with peacocks and roses,
across the gauze curtain around the bed.

There was a stoneware jar filled with rose water
on the tiled floor, tiles which had been there for a long time,
since the Greeks, the Phoenicians, perhaps earlier.
Do you remember the ships in the harbor
and the cacti climbing the hill
and the bare branches
of the olive and almond trees
(it was winter)
and the bell in the Norman tower
ringing six times
and the rock pigeon
that settled on the windowsill
and strutted back and forth
making cooing noises
until you shooed it away
with your hand, laughing
and saying that it should have been a hunting hawk
or that you wanted a hunting hawk or would I buy one for you?
Something like that. A coin or two
left on the bedside table wasn't going to be enough
for someone as good as you. You made that clear to me right away.

But how could you remember?
1,390 years is a long time, and you've
been through so many cycles since then,
manifesting yourself as a seagull, a puma, a butterfly, an ant...
And I forget. A white elephant of the Emir of Al-Rumaylah?
An orange carp swimming in a pool in the Imperial City in Peking?

You were fifteen. I was nineteen.
You were knowledgeable. You were accomplished.
You knew what to do. You guided me. You guided me in.
It was my first time. I didn't know what to expect.
Entering you was like pushing
against the bronze door of a palace
and stepping inside to find in the stone courtyard
a single two-handled vessel, an amphora from Corinth,
filled with perfume or wine or... Whatever. Some drug.
I was a soldier and you were... What? You never told me.
That was part of the mystery of it: you never told me.
What was that lotion I rubbed into your skin?
What did it have in it to make my head spin that way
as I licked you all over and kissed the back of your neck?
And how do you say "angelic curls" in Italian?
And what did you whisper in my ear and in what language?
You knew more than one. Malta was only a stop on the way for you.

I could say that I died six months later in Palestine
storming some castle or of cholera or in a tavern brawl
fighting over some boy who reminded me of you.
But the fact is, I lived to be 47,
dying on the island of Formentera,
in a whitewashed stone house with black shutters
above the Mediterranean Sea and the ships from Arabia
and the new religions and all those wars and all those corpses
of young men and the sleek horses and the greyhounds from Egypt.

I want to say that I remembered you all my life
and died with your name on my lips--gleecheenay!--
but there must have been long periods of time
when I didn't remember you at all. I had a busy life.
And you forgot me before you crossed through
the marketplace that sparkling, cold winter morning
on your way to some other tryst with some other soldier,
perhaps an officer this time. You had your living to earn.
But I will say that your image returned to me periodically.
After all, you were my first time. A man always remembers
the first time. I still remember it, 1,390 years later
and who can count the number of incarnations since?

John

The incredible power of words. Warren writes much like you do. There is a similarity in the rhythm and intensity of your poetry. I save them all, they are exquisite.

JoAnn

I find it interesting that this reader, JoAnn, finds similarities between the poetry of Warren and my poetry. Maybe there's more to all of this than even I realized. But if Warren has been loving me through my language or making love to me through my language as he says in his poem for ten years, then if there is a similarity in our work, perhaps it can be explained that way. This is a new kind of love affair and I didn't even have to go to a bar and cruise anybody. I just had to write poems and send them out on the internet. I just had to fling them out there like Whitman's noiseless, patient spider. It is nice to be loved for my language and through my language. What more could any writer ask for?

John

Some of Us

Some of us are in love every day of our lives
with someone or something. We have these passions--
for that boy tossing that football or delivering that pizza
or getting into that red Mustang or bent over that electric guitar.
Or if it's not a boy it's for something nobody ever heard of--
Shostakovich or Paul Klee or Alyosha Karamazov.
We're so weird. We'd go to the prom with Stan if they'd let us.
We're the ones who in junior high school write the name Chuck
or Frankie on the cover of our algebra book and draw a heart
around it and the palms of our hands get sweaty and people
look at us sideways and teachers we do not know
are closet lesbians glance knowingly at us and then away.
It isn't all sexual though it is mostly sexual
as the sun in its explosions is mostly sexual
and the feeling of summer on the backs of our hands
or the sand of a beach in August under our bare feet
or shingles on a barn roof under our fingertips
or tar on a country road. Hot. Like that. Love
is like that. And we embody it. Yes.
Others are off somewhere doing something useful,
making money, making babies, joining the Marines.
But we're in love--with someone, with something
every day of our lives. Passionate
like an almond blossom or a peach.
Men in positions of authority
look down from pulpits or lecterns
and tell us that God is love, which is puzzling,
because we've also been told, often by the same men,
that God doesn't love us, hates us in fact, and wants us dead.
But we're so intensely alive inside, burning with this love thing.
It's like a light. It's dangerous. How to turn it off?
Where's the switch? For us there is no switch.
We could be killed. Others are. It's terrifying.
How to make what's hot into something cold
and be like other men--
flat-faced, gold rimmed glasses, briefcase, Bible, money in the bank,
wife and two kids (a girl and a boy and the boy plays with dolls)
and the house on Mockingbird Lane and the black Buick in the garage.
But not for us. We're out there on the edge, dancing.
We're up there in the stratosphere, dreaming.
We're shining in the darkness. Like a lamp on a bedside table.
Like the light through the bamboo shade.

And through the petals of the Japanese iris in the vase.
Reflected off the porcelain. Off the mirror on the wall.
Off the burning candle. Off the wings of the blue moth
attracted to the flickering, insidious flame.

Falling in love again.
Never wanted to.
What am I to do?
I can't help it.

John

Reasons Why I Need A Boyfriend

because the pillows
which were once on my bed
and which I used to cuddle with
pretending they were my boyfriend
have run off together
and left me alone

because my bed
which once had pillows
is now much too big
to fall asleep in
without someone next to me

because I can't bring myself
to actually break down and submit
a personal romance ad
although I have a stack
in this drawer to my left
that I have written
for that very purpose

because I want to write poetry
love poetry, to be exact
and not the good kind
that people will be reading for decades
but the mushy, sappy, sickeningly sweet
bad poetry
that would probably rhyme
and end up on greeting cards
decorated with generic red hearts
rainbows
and roses

but mostly because
when I am driving through the desert
as I am doing right now
and the sky is clear
and I pull over to look at the stars
and the full moon
illuminates the landscape
I have no one to dance with.

Warren

Eros

Warren, the god that's tormenting you is Eros, which seems appropriate somehow. You are a young and beautiful person who is either always subject to Eros or sad because you are not subject to Eros at the present moment. Of all the people I have ever met, you need to be in love every minute of your young life. It seems to me that this is who you are, this is where you're at.

Yesterday we talked about "a classical education" and I can see where it would be useful here because there is what we call a "myth," a classical myth, which would fit your situation and even though I am an educated person I don't know what that myth is because I did not study Greek and Latin. It's probably in Ovid's Amores. I know where it is but not what it is. There are worse fates than being subject to Eros though. It can be pleasant at least part of the time. To be in love is nice. For you it is essential.

I wrote a poem for you about this after you visited here and will now find it and post it.

John

I Have Everyone To Dance With

Because
I have no one
to dance with,
I have everyone
to dance with.
I call it
the dance of emptiness.
I call it
the dance of nothingness.
I call it
the dance of the void.
Notice how
the idling of the car engine
and the headlights
glowing
in the late night mist
and my bare feet on the floor
and my hand on the steering wheel
and my eyes on the sky
and the star dunes around me
and the ocotillo
with its spiny stems and scarlet
blossoms
and the tiny elf owl
peering
out of the saguaro cactus
and each individual
grain of sand
filling each footprint of each
coyote and wild burro
and the waning moon
and the planet Mars
and the scorpion and the snake
and the Gila Mountains
waking into light
and the black Pinacate volcano field
turning white
and this pencil
which I have lifted
from the dashboard
and this map of Arizona
which I took from the seat beside me

and this poem
which I'm writing
on this map
at this exact moment
in my life—
all
rush in
to fill the space.

John

On Becoming Famous

I've been thinking, for days now, about the posts you sent out a few days back about not "being famous". Here is my thought on the subject – you have achieved something that surpasses fame. By that I mean, you reach people on a level so much higher, and so much more important, than you would through fame.

No, you aren't selling a million copies of a book. Maybe they only sell one at a time or 10 in a month or whatever the number may be. But every person who reads those words, every person who reads your poems on the internet, is forever changed by them. If you don't believe it, ask me. Ask Jesse. Ask Kameron. I could go on. Hell, ask any person you know! This is such a higher goal to reach. To impact and forever change a reader who finds your words ... this should be the goal of every writer who seeks to publish.

It's not about the numbers, not about the interviews, not about the talk shows. It's about the readers. And I'm willing to bet that most people who read what you write *want* to tell you personally how much you have changed their life. Only a few know how to seek you out.

Warren

Famous

Several weeks have gone by
in which I haven't envied Naomi Shihab Nye,
haven't thought about being rich and famous,
haven't wanted to be Merwin, W.S. or Heaney, Seamus,
haven't imagined myself Yusef Komunyakaa or Robert Hass,
not to mention Boy George or Mama Cass,
Krsto Hegedusic or Carolyn Kizer.
Have I've gotten older and wiser?
Who'd want to be Robert Lowell, Robert Pinsky or Robert Bly,
red-faced and strangling in a Rooster tie,
and a Brooks Brothers button-down and Cole-Haan shoes,
reading my ho-hum poems on the Snooze Hour (snooze)
or winning the Nobel or the Pulitzer,
or with an audience of millions like Wolf Blitzer?
I'd rather limit my audience to one or two,
especially if they're cute and smart and loving – like you.

John

The Loss of Twenty-Two Pots in a Meltdown

Though this is a terrible loss,
try to take it in a Buddhist way.
The twenty-two pots were an illusion.
Loss gives us the opportunity
to see loss as an illusion
and to look through loss
into non-essential emptiness.
What is the color
of non-essential emptiness?
What is its chemical composition?
Where did the smoke go
when it stopped being smoke?
What did the fire say
after it stopped being fire?
How much nothingness
can meltdown contain?
What is the taste
of meltdown on the tongue?
If the twenty-two pots
were the gay male chorus
of Glendale, Arizona
which Cole Porter song
would they not be singing?
How many metallic pings
would the song not contain?
How would the song end
if it had no ending?
How many beginnings
would the song have
if it had no beginning?
What is the sound of sound
when it is the absence of sound?

John

The Line Part of You Goes Out to Infinity

"The line part of you goes out to infinity."
– Ron Padgett, *Reading Reverdy*

The desert has a wrinkled face of cold gold-gray.
My friend Warren's in bed this clear winter Sunday.

Tomorrow I'm going to send him an object trove.
My friend: like little Lord Jesus asleep in the hay.

Life is complicated and it's often difficult being gay.
All the New York School poets read Pierre Reverdy.

America can break your heart. Alas and lackaday.
My friend's eyes are opening now. O my castaway!

A love without an object burning night and day.
I lifted that line from a poem by Pierre Reverdy.

Love, the object is everywhere. Start your day.
I'm thinking of you. And reading Pierre Reverdy.

John

A Question

Has your life up this point been a success?

John

An Answer

Resoundingly: YES!

I'm creating, which adds to the beauty of the universe, even if no one other than myself ever sees the creations. I pour love out in every direction. John can attest to this. I love everyone, even many that I probably shouldn't. I'm not living on the street, I have a nice apartment that I enjoy coming home to every night. I have a job that doesn't pay much, but allows me to pay my bills and interact with new and interesting people every day.

I am writing, I am drawing, I am painting, I am working with clay and sculpture and glass. I feel good about myself. To me, this means success. I feel centered, unwanting, content. I recognize the mistakes and bad moments I have had in the past and probably will encounter in the future and I embrace those moments and mistakes as life lessons. I would not undo a single event, because it would cost me a lesson which has helped to make me the person I am today. So, yes. *Resoundingly, YES!*

Warren

How Sweet It Is

My first action after waking up on this brilliantly sunlit summer morning was to call up and print out Warren's *YES!* and thumbtack it to the wall behind this computer, thumbtack it right next to the mask he sent me, the Little Boy Blue mask. I can see the printed out message by simply looking up over the top edge of this computer. There it is – *a resounding YES!*

A resounding *YES!* to remind me that we were made for love and that our ability to love can be extended toward art and toward writing and toward philosophy and toward music and toward science--and toward life and love. And *YES!* – "They can't take that away from me." And yes, "An army of creators can never be defeated!" And *YES!* as Pirsig says in Zen and the Art of Motorcycle Maintenance, "People notice Quality and they respond to it and we are then never without friends who understand and who also create along with us." Then we are on the side of life and we wake up in sunlight and the first word to tumble off our lips is – *YES!* As that great philosopher Jackie Gleason used to say every Saturday night on the new Philco fifty years ago -- *"How sweet it is!"*

We are having another raku firing this morning and I've said I'd be there at eight before the heat makes firing a raku kiln uncomfortable. But I wanted to say the above before I start my day. Thank you, Warren the Wordman.

John

How Sweet It Is

I saw a grinning boy
sitting on a pink cloud,
and he laughed and said,
"We've been around the Wheel
many times, me and you,
we've died as chrysanthemums
and come back as sparrow hawks,
expired as Basho and been reborn
as Shelley, drunk small beer with
Marlowe and eaten beef with Whitman.
But this is the best incarnation yet."
And I realized the boy was you.
And I realized the joy I felt was you.

John

And In Closing ...

_____

How I Feel About Warren

I love you like the younger brother I never really had. I do have a younger brother. He lives in Chicago. But in the sixty years of his life we have never had a single moment of meaningful contact. I've only seen him perhaps three times in the last forty years. One time (at my father's funeral) I didn't even recognize him or know who he was. I am, however, very close to my sister. Still, to me, you are the younger brother I never had.

I have loved you since you sat on my couch last winter clutching the pillow to your chest as you talked just as I clutch the pillow to my chest when I talk. There is something so vulnerable about clutching a pillow to your chest and so protective and perhaps also defensive, though when I questioned you about it you said it wasn't defensive. And I said, "I do it because it keeps my chest warm." "I do it because when I lie down to read a book I can prop the book up on the pillow."

I love you because after seeing the interior of my house, with its art, you elected to take art classes. I love you because one of your drawings is on the wall behind this computer above the photograph of Al C. between Randy Weeks and the musician in the trio from Switzerland. A drummer, I think.

If I maintain that doing your art--even if doing it is an absurd existential act and can be meaningful only to you as an artist and then only at that exact moment of creation and not later – I am thinking of you, and it's because I love you. And if you stop doing art – even if you create art only for yourself – the whole world suffers. I mean, if we can believe that the flicking of a butterfly's wings in Seattle can within a week cause storms off the coast of Patagonia, then we can believe that if the creation of your art stops in Phoenix someone dies of a bullet wound in Mali next month.

I love you because you are always falling in love. I always fall in love, also. I love so many people it breaks my heart when, for reasons beyond my control, I lose them--as I have lost Jason, whose cup broke two days ago, and apparently Wendell, though I'm not sure. I simply have not heard from him in several weeks and he did indicate he was angry at me for being "privileged," whatever that means. One cannot as a gay man walk out on friends and stop communicating with them this way. If being gay means anything it has to mean loving other men. Especially now, we each need to affirm that we love men. Dumping friends, putting the phone off the hook, moving on without a forwarding address, doing "attitude," rejecting people, not staying for breakfast, not saying, "I love you" –. That was yesterday. This is today. This is what it means today to be gay.

I love you because we went into the Tibetan shop on 18th Street in San Francisco and I bought that change purse. They make change purses in Tibet? Yes, they weave them of different colored yarns, yellow, red, black. I love you because I was taking you on the John Tour and I went over with you to High Gear but then, if you remember, we didn't stay there more than a minute and I sent you on your way toward love and adventure. I love you because taking you to my clothing store like that was a way of saying, "I value this store. I want to share it with you. It's a quality store." That store is gone now, closed down, out of business. But the reason the owner gave was that he was tired of running it. He didn't close down because anyone increased the rent. I love you because every time I take that change purse out to pay for lunch at Jerre-Anne's World Famous I think of the moment I bought it and the fact that I was with you and it reaffirms the love I feel for you, my little brother I never had till I was lucky enough to meet you.

I love you because we sat on the wall of my favorite view spot and looked out at The Mission and I said, "This is my favorite view spot. I'm sharing it with you. I want you to have it, also." Especially now. Because, given conditions, I can't get to that view spot. We need to carry these images in our minds and cherish them. Because when we lose the friend we were with--and in the next 10 years I am going to lose 50 percent of my friends through death because many of them are old now, including Larry – we have also compromised the memory, the vision in the mind, the moment of love and affirmation and sharing and being together. We have to maintain that moment. That's one of the things that love is all about: sharing the moment, sharing the vision, and then maintaining it by fighting to preserve it as long as life endures. After life ends, well, if we've captured the moment in a poem or drawing, the moment endures longer, doesn't it?

That the straight guy can say he loves you is a breakthrough event for him. Remain his friend while life endures.

John

Without You

The elixirs on the pharmacist's shelf would cash in their crystals.
Every electric boat in Santa's workshop would forget how to toot.
Words like *magnetic* and *trance* would vanish from the language.
The raindrops that *boink-boink* on the window sill would go still.
Holstein cows would be bereft in the sunflower fields of Kansas.

John

www.ingramcontent.com/pod-product-compliance
Lightning Source LLC
Chambersburg PA
CBHW020347290526
45785CB00005B/2180